# Amber's Big Dog

Margaret Ryan
Illustrated by Jan Smith

It was Amber's birthday.
She wanted a dog.

So Amber, Pete, Mum and
Dad went to the dogs' home.

"I like this little dog," said Dad.

"I like this little dog," said Mum.

"I like this little dog," said Pete.

"I love this big dog," said Amber.

"That big dog will eat a lot," said Amber's dad.

"That big dog will want lots of walks," said Amber's mum.

"I will look after the big dog," said Amber. "Please can we have him?"

So they took the big dog home.

The next day, Amber took the big dog for a walk in the park.
The big dog ran off.
"Stop! Stop! Wait for me!" shouted Amber.

Then the big dog jumped up at a man.
"Oh, no!" said Amber.

Then the big dog jumped in a pond.
"Oh, no!" said Amber.

At the end of the walk, Amber was tired, but the big dog wasn't.

When she got home, Amber had an idea.
She got her go-cart out of the shed.

Amber put the dog in front of the go-cart. Then she got in.

They went to the park. The big dog pulled the go-cart along.
The big dog got tired but Amber didn't.
"What a good idea!" said everyone.